Nominy-Dominy

Lesley Saunders has written eight poetry collections, most recently the chapbook *Angels on Horseback* (smith|doorstop, 2017), and has performed at festivals and on the radio. Winner of many awards for her work, Lesley has collaborated with artists, photographers, sculptors, dancers, and a composer and choir. A reviewer, editor, mentor and workshop leader, she holds visiting professorships at UCL Institute of Education, and Newman University, Birmingham.

Other books by the same author:

The Dark Larder, Corridor Press (1997)
Christina the Astonishing with Jane Draycott & Peter Hay, Two Rivers Press (1998)
Her Leafy Eye with Geoff Carr, Two Rivers Press (2009)
No Doves, Mulfran Press (2010)
Cloud Camera, Two Rivers Press (2012)
The Walls Have Angels, Mulfran Press (2014)
Periplous: the Twelve Voyages of Pytheas, Shearsman Books (2016)
Angels on Horseback, smith|doorstop (2017)

Also by Two Rivers Poets:

David Attwooll, *The Sound Ladder* (2015)
Kate Behrens, *The Beholder* (2012)
Kate Behrens, *Man with Bombe Alaska* (2016)
Adrian Blamires, *The Pang Valley* (2010)
Adrian Blamires & Peter Robinson (eds.), *The Arts of Peace* (2014)
David Cooke, *A Murmuration* (2015)
Terry Cree, *Fruit* (2014)
Claire Dyer, *Eleven Rooms* (2013)
Claire Dyer, *Interference Effects* (2016)
A. F. Harrold, *The Point of Inconvenience* (2013)
Ian House, *Nothing's Lost* (2014)
Gill Learner, *The Agister's Experiment* (2011)
Gill Learner, *Chill Factor* (2016)
Sue Leigh, *Chosen Hill* (2018)
Becci Louise, *Octopus Medicine* (2017)
Mairi MacInnes, *Amazing Memories of Childhood, etc.* (2016)
Steven Matthews, *On Magnetism* (2017)
Henri Michaux, *Storms under the Skin* translated by Jane Draycott (2017)
Tom Phillips, *Recreation Ground* (2012)
John Pilling and Peter Robinson (eds.), *The Rilke of Ruth Speirs:*
    New Poems, Duino Elegies, Sonnets to Orpheus & Others (2015)
Peter Robinson, *English Nettles and Other Poems* (2010)
Peter Robinson (ed.), *Reading Poetry: An Anthology* (2011)
Peter Robinson (ed.), *A Mutual Friend: Poems for Charles Dickens* (2012)
Peter Robinson, *Foreigners, Drunks and Babies: Eleven Stories* (2013)
Robert Seatter, *The Book of Snow* (2016)
Susan Utting, *Fair's Fair* (2012)
Susan Utting, *Half the Human Race* (2017)
Jean Watkins, Scrimshaw (2013)

Nominy-Dominy

Lesley Saunders

TWO
RIVERS
PRESS

First published in the UK in 2018 by Two Rivers Press
7 Denmark Road, Reading RG1 5PA.
www.tworiverspress.com

ISBN 978-1-909747-34-0

1 2 3 4 5 6 7 8 9

Two Rivers Press is represented in the UK by Inpress Ltd
and distributed by NBNi.

Cover design by Sally Castle with a painting by Peter Hay
Text design by Nadja Guggi and typeset in Janson and Parisine

Printed and bound in Great Britain by Imprint Digital, Exeter

Acknowledgements

Thanks are due to the editors of the following journals, anthologies and
websites who first published some of the poems in this book, including *Ambit*,
Areté, *Forward Prize Anthology*, Corinium Museum, *Divers*, *Eborakon*, *Frogmore
Papers*, *Live Canon Prize anthology 2015*, *London Review of Books*, *Magma*, the
Manchester Poetry Prize website, *New Hall Lives II*, *New Poetries VI* (Carcanet),
Poetry London, *Poetry Salzburg Review*, *Scintilla*, *The New Statesman*, *The North*,
the Reading Poetry Festival website, *The Arts of Peace* (Two Rivers Press),
The Rialto, and *Warwick Review*.

My thanks are also due to Helen McNeil, Bridget Somekh and members
of the Subversifs poetry group for their comments on earlier versions of some
of the poems, and especially to Linda Saunders for her invaluable advice on
the collection as a whole. Peter Robinson at Two Rivers Press has been both
a thorough and a hugely supportive editor throughout.

For my teachers

'Ibant obscuri sola sub nocte per umbram
Perque domos Ditis vacuas et inania regna'
—Vergil, *Aeneid VI*, 268–9

To all the gods, one amphora of honey.
To the Mistress of the Labyrinth(?), one amphora of honey.
—Mycenaean Tablet KN Gg702

It was a time marked from beginning to end by calamity.
But it was also the time men would go on dreaming of,
long after that fire had gone out.
—Roberto Calasso, *The Marriage of Cadmus and Harmony*

Contents

II. Ora Maritima | 35

III. 'And the smoke of it fragrant with spices' | 73

I.
The Uses of Greek

Oxyrhynchus

'The past is never dead. It's not even past.'

Rootling around in rubbish dumps
I've accumulated a seam of filth
beneath each fingernail, oh precious

objects, prodigies. The body speaks.
A week's dirty dishes hurl themselves
at the wall, it's harder these days

(the dark isn't nearly dark enough)
to get to the bottom of things, for dirt
to be what it is, passionate and smudged,

unaloof. No wonder I wake-dream
of all the unpaired earrings, the heap
of muttering papyri, polymorphous

mud-slingers, witnesses to the damage
I must name and own; the gamey smell
on my skin is its appetite, massive, amok.

Horse

It's the year of the horse:
wood horse. War or no
it is a comforting thought
to be pregnant, quick
with sharp-elbowed men

the whole gang of them agog
and jostling to be birthed
in this back street no midwife
one dog barking grave of night.
Earth horse. The woman

is comfort of a different kind
her *femme fatale* hands
on the nicked hide of the taut belly
her slow voice in the pricked ears
of the trembling foal:

Dare alla luce. Fire horse –
smoke billowing over balconies
like blown silk.
On the shore the white waves
water horse

rocking to and fro
between fish-dazzle, tin-flash.
Then drumbeat blank verse
man–beast coupling: metal
horse. My iron-hooved sons.

Terrorist

Bronze figurine with gold earrings and a spiral torque,
Colchis, 3rd century BCE

Going down on their knees to kiss the warm throat
of the earth after the calamity years *polyphloisboio thalassēs*
their first words to their wives turning all that fury and hurt
to furs and gold, the old campaigners know nothing of satiety,

their orgasmic homecomings just another leg of the journey.
Battalions of bad boys in a landscape of bare rock and riddles
are what they do best, one-night stands with easy foreign girls,
day-trips to hell. The ram's fleece was part of it,

along with the dragon-teeth and WMD, tall tales,
an oblivion of cheap drink. Trying to obliterate
the lost continent of earrings in the form of birds,
the way she pushed her words towards him across the floor,

how she pulls off her petals, the way she cries like a lamb
in wolf's clothing. How it will all end in war.

Fray

We at home want some good news. More casualties
are diagnosed, the foxholes of the body
are a black box of tricks, a cradle
of pains. Old friends have been posting letters

full of protocols: aloud they sound like sung
recitations of the Homeric virtues
we thought, in the flower of our lives,
we'd never need. Lymph nodes and bone marrow:

this soldiers' kit of clean lint and safety pins
with its bedside voice and brave face. O my loves.
The magnolia, shorn of petals
in a late frost; these invisible harms.

A Private Woman

'For the first time in her life, Helen was not being pestered
by men. One day she was lying, daydreaming, in the bath
when some serving-maids burst in disguised as Erinyes...'

A locked door, the red Turkish curtain
draped over a blank wall.
Daybed, its candlewick cover not lain on.
In the corner of my eye

there was once a visitor
gleaming with beauty and raiment

who arrived with his leg-wound, his war-poem.
I was watching my life
through globes of sea-glass,
haloes of rock-salt and wrack.

No mirror here now but the night-window,
no gilt-framed portraits, only a tin boat

and a pile of grey pebbles
beached up on the bathroom floor
and I, *terrified the storm will snatch me up again,*
will carry me weeping over the fish-filled sea,

how I wish I could hide my incurable hair, my marriages,
my borrowed crimes under these tiles.

Tiresias

A week after his wife died he became a woman.

More than her frocks or the stockings like skin
to the touch, more than the hairbrush weft with her hair

she left by the bed, more even than the long-playing record
of her silvery voice in his phone, was the knowledge
that he'd loved her without having known how it felt

to be loved so much, to the depths, to be clutched
too hard to his hungry breast. Unmanned by grief
he sniffs her flagons of gone-off scent, buffs his fingernails,

takes a razor to the fuzz on his legs; dyes his hair red
the shade of hers when they met. Later, the palest pout
of her lipstick; an artless smear of mascara. Very soon

he'll know everything, the language of goldfinches,
wrens; he feels he could fly. Rare as an oryx,
he could go without nourishment into the Sahara,

solitary and widowed, unicorn, recluse – dwell in her
for aeons, till the dark of his sorrow is milk and stars,

seven lifetimes not enough for such quickening.

Army Musician

Enveloped in wet turf
all these bloodless years
like a vellum psalter
or ancestral soul,
deaf to muffled voices
of rescuers overhead,
a six-inch frame drum
surfaces through a sky
of mud, moon-faced,
its veiled questions
how long from, how far since
and whether it was morning
or afternoon when the tune
in his head deserted him
like a flight of quail
or shooting stars; whether
he could then or afterwards
in the march-past of silences,
magnificent, tobacco-laden,
in the spent blue of evening,
all fifes and bugles gone,
have cut a makeshift whistle
from a horsetail-reed
or fathomed the actions
of small heroic birds wheeling
and manoeuvring
in the pools of air
a hair's-breadth above him.

Helmet

'autik' apo kratos koruth' heileto phaidimos Hektor'

for my grandson aged one

Its eyes are empty but the brows are wingspans
eagling over the low skies of the helmet's gaze

where tomorrow's battlefield sprawls. No wonder
the child is terrified. The bronze rings out,

a thick male voice sounding through the mask,
Wotan, Jehovah, Ogun. This is not the father

you love, the one with gifting hands and the look
of blue daylight all round him. But if the cap fits

you will learn this new language, how grave and gold
it tastes, inlaid with garnets and sagas, sunburnt,

sumptuous with works and days, you will see
with its eyes how gallantly the world is made.

Shield

'I have no armour left, you have stripped it from me.'

for Michael Hulse

Where are the footholds in this hard surface,
the sea-roads or star-maps,
and what do we women know of war,
its prosthetic arts and glacial edges

or whose mailed hands have stripped
the heart-leaved bougainvillea from our porch?

A mother plants her body – all its ploughed fields,
its blood price and bridal procession, its city
of labyrinths, its straight-horned heifers
and white barley loaves, its bluish vine-fruits

and the flute-voiced boy – between her son
and his fate. What we noticed was the absence

of yellow roses, the lack of gift-embroideries
or kiss-words on the threshold of his awaking:
the inner side of the shield is a pane
where he can see the polished blank of his face,

its stubborn bronze and tin and incorruptible gold.
He thinks of the flies in his friend's dead flesh,

the oiled and tasselled hair gazed at from behind
when he was living and strong. Then Achilles
walked along the shore of the sea, crying a terrible cry
for the slain, the sons and fathers of them.

The gleam of those urns and lace-edged table-napkins
were our first books of light, those hurt shining words.

Aurum

We grunt like slaves, blackened, naked to the waist,
sweating in the alembic of the mountain – as if
King Agamemnon's cries had only just now died away,
and smiths were being summoned to the reeking palace
to remake his face in a sheet of beaten metal.
Nothing changes. Light falls on the seam, and all is
heave and scrabble; we are lead dreaming ourselves
otherwise, our own magnum opus, forked trove.

Olfactory

'Shall you have no pity for me?'

As he basked in that Aegean island noon,
the ocean brochure-azure, asphodels glossy
and stiff as symbols, he didn't need to pluck
at his shirt, stick his nose in his pits to know
it was him: source of volatile organic compounds,
mobile oil-factory of sun-rotted whale,
first in the telegenic line of embarrassing bodies.
The leaflets in Greek that dropped on the shingle

were telling him to pack his kit, make ready for Troy
after all. The sense of smell fatigues quickly
he hopes, though he knows from his *temps perdu*
how shocking the odour of bodies can be,
Herakles' sweat on his flesh, the salt-fish
stink of his sex, still washing over him in waves
of longing, disgust. He tries to classify its notes:
pungent, musky, camphoraceous, *kai ta loipa*

– and what about the menthol-madeleine moment
of shared cigarette, silk-cut on linked fingers,
sweet reek of love? His foot aches inexpressibly,
clostridium perfringens eating his gristle, tendons,
his pedestrian bones, reworking them as gangrene, stench.
It was the snake, a poisoned arrow, the consequence
of chronic smoking, it was vengeance or penance,
it was quitting or failure to quit, it was a curse

or a cure in itself. It was him.

Nociception

'Ah, ah, ah, ah!'

And as he lay there on Lemnos
tethered by ineffable pain
under the hatless branches of a thorn-tree
he remembered the doctor-philosophers
and their futile attempts at description
in terms of temperature, shape, colour:
as in, the countess's jewel-headed pins,
some winged thing, arc-lit, charred,

a stem of antimony bitten to the quick,
a triangle of silver cruets glimpsed
without warning from the sunken garden
as a chandelier floods on,
a dozen blood-red epiphanies,
any solitaire quilt
thrown round a swiftly-executed *contrapaso*,
the murderous taste of glass music

– whatever is left, no matter how implausible
or smart-arsed, must be the truth,
even though these are only some of the winters,
only some of the brain-scans and heartbreaks,
some of the shooter-slugs or director's cuts,
some of the wounds, womanish and stinking,
only some of the stolen violins,
are only some of the windows he walked through

trying to describe in his own words how it felt.

Ransom

The art of losing face was a gift
he must have learned young,
how to turn down the heat of his gaze,
bring the blood up to his cheeks,

summon the shame. In later years
he'd lose the other stuff, heart, looks,
footing, all done with grace.
A hero not of our time,

his knees turned to quiver and piss
that day the god crept too close,
hat tilted over one eye,
wings and beak under a hood.

Now fame, glory, honour gone,
he sees there's no such thing as lost,
men are foundlings, all. On his knees,
King Priam begs for the body of his son.

Sack

after Vergil

café culture street life quis cladem illius noctis a woman in her twenties wearing a fur-collared coat quis funera fando explicet had been drinking in a bar close by aut possit lacrimis aequare labores it was a concert where the music was loud plurima perque vias sternuntur a girl was carried by a young man in his arms inertia passim corpora she appeared to be dead crudelis ubique luctus, ubique pavor people were panicked, wounded, screaming, blood was running all over them et plurima mortis imago they were all so young Coroebus Rhipeus Hypanis Dymas Panthus I was on the ground with a man on top of me and another one beside me up against a wall I don't know how long we stayed like that urbs antiqua ruit it seemed like an eternity

Assay

'I thought I saw gold behind it.'

What is it draws you here to its cypress gardens
and sarcophagi? An arched foot, an archaic smile,
splendour of breastplates in the long afternoon
and the fatigues of dusk, half-heard hostage-songs?

Or – like the sun's scant gram of pallid gold
buried in war-cloud the colour of guns –
Helen's diadem, her labrys-earrings and anklets,
a wrought gilt cup and the dulled knife blades,

all hidden under the hill? Weigh them in your palm,
in the balance, the troy ounces of precious metal,
love and wrath, win or death, pence for the ferry.
(The light on the plain was sapphire, faceted,

the earlobes pierced and waiting, the wet sand
a cemetery of pearls.) Or something else entirely?

Trophy

after 'Sophia Schliemann wearing the Jewels of Helen'

You must have thought it had your name on it
like the cry of a child for its mother in the dark,

the gold mass slipping backwards out of the soil,
a breech birth into the open arms of your shawl.

Or so he said. Girl-bride, you were in Athens
sprinkling earth on the family grave, the shadows

under your eyes still showing even after he loaded
the diadem on your head, locked the heavy collar –

and so you will always be Helen, looking out to sea,
Troy in ruins, and the orphan gold in no-man's land.

Immortal Daughters

'... for we still have your immortal daughters, your songs'

I hang for this delightful season
like a crêpe de chine shift
on detachable shoulders –
diaphanous folds of seemingness
in the hero's house while police
digging in a garden find another

Rapt in my tissue
in my parchment
I am fingered by scholars
shaking me out like a butterfly
exclaiming over my syntax of desire
[bad girl] while a man in a balaclava

I have a beautiful daughter
my golden blossom of being
whom I would not

I found a syllable
under the wind's tongue
and netted it with my barbitos
my words were open-mouthed
I exhaled strange dialects

A gust of desire shook me
to my roots, a deranged tree
in a mountain storm
I long for you always
absence my substance
[but my face was once on a coin]

I have a daughter [but
the man with a gun]
I have a syllable [but
they say my husband]
here is my slim petticoat
[I will go without breakfast]

I am scattered through the books
of grammarians, rotting
on a rubbish dump [bad girl
to have had her own rhymes &]

do not say that I am dead
someone will remember us
the ivied mountain will be waiting
and the men who have parsed us
will eat the bad meat of these leaking
words my daughter

Landfall

'... Charaxon elthen
naï sun plēai...'

One can imagine a brother. I played alone
in a back garden far from the sea among
my father's roses; jet trails feathered
the endless summer sky,

daylight sailed the coastline of my room.
I prayed at night though not for him,
out there in the deep of a universe
whose horizons swerved

far beyond the reach or sway of any mercy
I could think of. After roses, the blue
and gold of asters, cold stars to navigate
the year's vast tides by.

There's a name for what I feel, though
I don't know it yet, my Greek still falters
over words for unharvested, heart-heavy.
        Barythymia: all at sea.

Mare Internum

*'... we work with fragments, we work with dreams,
we work with the longing for lost texts to be discovered,
for every broken thing to be repaired...'*

The sea-road thunders, spume-lash and wind-slap
      crack against canvas, peeling the eyes, parching lips,
piercing the ears' skin; a mind strains to surface
      somewhere, but the journey's purpose has long
been drowned – jute-trade, was it, or herrings,
      or perhaps even a war; or just curiosity and the hope
that it would all be different away from home
      (a man once, stripped and sodden, kissed the soil
where he landed, threw himself to the ground
      and sobbed out the remnants of his shipwrecked soul,
then slept in the bracken, its pungent smell close
      and warm in his nostrils, in his ears the muffled
booming of the tide, and over it a lone tern's wail).
      Whatever it was hardly matters. The time
between the land that was left and the land
      that's to come tosses endlessly back and forth,
going nowhere. Days topple into dim darknesses
      and clamber up in pallid mists, reeling
and pitching from one bleached horizon to the next.
      Desolate days, fever days when names and nations
mean nothing and there is only sky and sea,
      sea and sky. After a drab exhausted dawn
an hour's truce, a plateau between wave-scarps
      when a mauvish-grey floats in the distance.
Land. Then the hissing waves rear up,
            close over, *thalassa thalassa*. Will sleep ever come
to us here on the far side of the world?

Praise Song for a Pair of Earrings

'Then Anchises by divine will and destiny
lay with the immortal goddess, the mortal, not knowing the truth of it...'

A man may be shipwrecked in a dozen different ways,
by how a far-off cloud resembles land, the longed-for
shore obscured by mist and glimmer; or by how

across a room of friends an unknown woman looks
at him a moment longer than she should – and so
a suitor may wait a lifetime for his lover. Or, maybe,

just this once, his luck is in: a goddess has fallen
for a mortal man. He's ready to believe whatever
she may tell him – that she's girlish, untouched

by love and all its dusky fingerings, its sweetest
of nothings. She'll be his bride. His hands tremble
as he fumbles with her girdle, trespassing, lingering,

then lifts the veil – god, her beauty is unbearable.
He shades his eyes from the blaze, the torcs and cuffs,
in her soft lobes the flower-buds of shimmering gold;

then the tumbling crown of hair. He knows, and chooses
not to know, the truth. From somewhere deep within
he cries her name, a wedding-bed is made, and history begins.

Genestho

'Let it be as I say.'

The reeds must be planted in a sluggish alkaline environment such as estuarial wetlands. After harvesting they must be split open and the pith stripped, arranged in layers, mashed. *Uag* grows on the isthmus where the palace of the Ptolemies rises like a huge dawn sun out of the ooze, looking out towards the sea of the Greeks. A scribe enters carrying a stack of documents. *Tjufi* is cheap and easy to produce, and stable in dry conditions: ideal for book-keeping, bills of sale et cetera. Canidius is asking for a kickback, tax breaks on his import and export business. Wreaths of the flower-umbels are laid as offerings on the coffins of the wealthy. Friends in high places. Her arms gleam with myrrh oil and thick silver bangles. She signs, hands the letter over. Weaver-birds nest in the sedge.

Prosopography

'Only the patterns... have any standing.'

i.m. Moses Finley

Though boundary stones have little to tell on their own, together
they're a story worth hearing: mortgage, tenure, credit, debt, land
as collateral. By coincidence someone else was busy writing it. But
'a friend does not lend; he gives'; and therein lies the difficulty –
among rustic villages and small farmsteads, allotments of broken
stumps and wild thyme, the sunburnt olive-bearing *oikoi* of
chieftains, ox-breeders, boat-builders, silver-smiths, gift-givers,
the name of the game is family and kinship, collective biographies
of immigrants and indigenes, slaves and fishmongers. The war, as
usual, intervened; Finkelstein changed his name in the year I was
born. To learn anything about the Greeks we have to approach
them backwards (is what he did not say). It's no bad thing to be a
king. He died the day after learning his wife was dead. There are
no immediate survivors.

Magna Graecia

Of course when they land in the harsh Sicilian afternoons they bring their wines and the art of fine dining with them. Also other gifts – the fig, the finger. In seaside towns and hill-villages, the womanly gesture of lifting the skirt averts the evil eye, ends rain, frightens gods, kills men. Flicking the chin shows how much you give a damn. The Greeks get everywhere, ghosts waist-deep in the ocean, slim figures plunging into the afterlife; the earrings, the cash. Marble fakes among sun-bleached ruins.

No-Name

'We call these things found even though they were not lost.'

back then the best that could be made
went down with the dead on their journey
the hours of single-minded bead-threading

axehead-grinding a way of finding closure
no doubt the bereaved turning themselves
to stone flint-faced practising emptiness

it was a way of life it was no way to live
every meal a full-scale expedition the fire
going out every time the wind gusted

no washing powder penicillin toothpaste
a taste for honey the exquisitest endorphin
salt its moreishness a cause for war

right on cue Odysseus the trick-cyclist
shows up with a pack of trouble-makers
eg Oedipus Zeno Socrates bringing gifts

very clever the climate having warmed up
the wine was appreciated also pelmanism
pretty baskets etc explosion of the arts

video of floating sea-shore island mirror
frontier then cut to cave safety dark one
eye on the future & management of change

no more forests just fields huge sky all
belly bread hold out both hands for more
but the double-eyed dead hungrier than ever

for the best that can be made FinePix™
of loved ones children playing in the mud
footprints who knows seven millennia ago

a way of finding closure perhaps or not
it was alright for Odysseus his journey
wife child I was the one with no name

The Uses of Greek

'...the acquisition of language is the only way of learning how to lose.'

for Marjorie Rigg, my mother-in-law and classical scholar,
who had Alzheimer's disease

i.
They went on with their meanings, oblivious –
it was part of their charm – of history's bric-a-brac;
unfazed by earthquakes in Agadir, the banging
of a shoe on a table in New York or the sudden fall
of *Poetry in Motion* from the top ten. The letters
settled in front of me like a cloud of chafers and fishmoths
crowding against a glass, just as they always had
and would: my favourites came last, χ's
elegant shears, bull-horned ψ, and φ that captained
all the words of love. In certain combinations, I learnt,
they might signify ritual murder in a palace bathroom,
a squaddie's first sight of the sea at the back end
of a mass retreat through Armenia, or the kiss
a homecoming husband gobs on the shining stones
as the roaring waves paw him ashore, a near-corpse,
a slither of clammy rags over the weeds.

ii.
In the beginning, we'd to master the palaver of armies –
their marches and manoeuvres, sieges and supplies,
a whisper of treachery in the mountain pass –
here were words doing duty as infantrymen, boxed
in phalanxes, safety in numbers, principal parts
on parade, commanding and being commanded.
But later, disobedient, dishevelled, they might surrender
to the inspiring breeze – leaves twittering on the holy oak,
mad semaphores. Here at last was somewhere to hide, deep
in between ἀάατος, inviolable and ὠώδης, egg-like, you could say
inscrutable. The boys I knew couldn't follow me there.

iii.
At the foot of the Acropolis
out in the open a man
sprang from nowhere, grabbed
at my breast – at twenty I had no syntax
of demurral, no μὴ μ' ἐρέθιζε
of classy defiance,
only an instinctive
horrified shove, the kind
of combat you learn
in the playground,
intimate and absurd.
Mainly I felt embarrassed
as if I'd been caught peeing
in public in this sacred place.
Whatever barbarians there are
are always within. And anyway
what use is Greek to a girl?

iv.
She's turned into something that looks like old shoes or bad dreams –
once she was taller than most of the men, tattoos on her arms,
livid stipples that imprinted her with the helix-horned deer;
in her thigh boots, in her silk burial dress she rode six horses
beyond the north wind through the feather-filled air where
Herodotus wrote there were griffins guarding the gold;
but when nothing can be written, everything's in the telling
and in her telling (we tell ourselves) she signed a way across
the trackless steppes, the endless inland archipelago set in a sea
of escaping memories. We need someone to tell our stories to,
someone to betray with each well-told tale, but who'll be the audience,
who the teller, who'll make sense of us, make history of us,
who'll disinter our dreams? What will we mean?

v.
Pregnant, I drove down to the holiday town one August afternoon
and stood on the promenade looking out to sea where he was,
in another country, ignorant. The high green swell was a comfort.
It answered the sea-sickness inside me, φεῦ τῆς βροτείας
φρενός and I thought of all the things that make us mortal,
all the moods and voices of λύω, to loosen or undo, as in
'to loose the maiden girdle after marriage', also to set free;
or, his knees were loosened in fear, and then: she loosed
the babe from her body. Love the limb-loosener.
Λέλυται πάντα, all is in confusion.

vi.
Parents and guardians teach us how to speak, though never quite
in words of our own choosing. (Find your voice, old poets
tell the young ones, as if you could get a life by trying.)
Like the Athens orator whose father made a living selling arms
we should go on stammering, we should practise speechifying
with pebbles in our mouths. Question: were the poets lying
before they spoke? Call no-one happy until dead, is good;
but don't you think they somehow gave us too much hope?
Don't you detect a congenital elegance in those cadences,
a knee-jerk need to choose the rightest word, when really
pain's tedious and banal and getting old means life's no longer
your own, a slippage into forgetfulness, filching tomatoes, falling,
falling, not wanting to get up, the rubber sheet under you?

vii.
No redemption then, just 'and the light's
blanked out'? Heaney gets it right –
no sin (so no forgiving), just fate
and worked-through past acts' weight –
but Harrison's déraciné too and maybe righter;
his Greek's rough-tough, a knife through butter:
'o o se toi... (bracket... bracket...)
where cows tread... (track it... track it...)'
Fragments of a plot we can't rediscover –
a way out, or through, a way to get some cover?
A choice between the self as knower, self as lover?

viii.
And mostly all there is are fragments; all
there is are mostly fragments, bright
surfaces that vibrate like splinters
of memory in the empty air, as if
in only a twinkling we were
... (in possession of?) ... pity...
trembling... old age now...
(my) skin... covers...
(Love?)...
flies pursuing (the young?)...
glorious... taking (your lyre?)
sing to us of the violet-robed one
... especially
... wanders...

ix.

This one's for muse numero nine, the last laugh,
the comic turn, the revolving door onto a naked case
of mistaken identity, the late-comer at the lit-fest,
the stand-up knock-down drop-dead art whose donkey's head
is one-size-fits-all, invisible to the wearer, now it's your turn.
In tragedy terror's on the surface, reconciliation's profound.
Comedy tells things another way round, the joke's on us,
you're the one telling it, but it's back to front and
you're the one telling it and you keep forgetting your lines
and time has stopped again and you're telling us we can
take a joke, oh Marjorie, what a laugh, what a hoot,
I could die laughing, did you know (of course you did)
there were once only three of them, Μελέτη, Μνήμη, Ἀοιδή,
meditation, memory, song? Two out of three ain't bad.
The opposite of memory is amnesia, also
amnesty. Who knows how much you had
to forgive, and what made you translate
to Leeds from Limavaddy where they'd a high opinion
of themselves? Clouds race across the sky in gales
of laughter, flowerbeds crack open in sly smiles,
the comedy of errors trips on, the bright surface
of things splits its sides, leaving us helpless, rocking
(in possession of?)... pity...
(Love?)...
...
...
sing to us... (?)
...

II.
Ora Maritima

Oral

The mouth-feel of Latin is anchovies,
as Greek's eucalyptus and burnt sugar,

simmered light. Latin is spatch-cock,
aquavit, scallion, partridge, crab-apple,

cud, gum. Greek is fig. On the tongue
is milk-thistle, muscat. Greek is eucharist,

orexic, crystal meth, Latin's breast-fed,
fellatious, al dente, wolfed. Picked clean.

Impasse

Elephants are easily terrified, the brightness
bouncing off the ice crystals burns their eyes.
Rome is still a week away down breakneck scarps

and frozen roads; half the corps are sick,
snow-blind and heart-sick. The light here is full
of damage, white, white, you must blacken

the skin beneath your eyes with charcoal lest
the glare, like a hawk who drives death into
a prey's brain with her middle claw, transfix you.

Some days we offer no resistance to the light,
we are stranded above the snowline, above
the drop, and our tears are unstoppable.

Comminus

Hand to hand. Like a man. The grip and creak of knuckles; knowing the precise moment to hold, let go. A blindfolded naked man, a man kneeling with his hands bound behind him, a man crowned, a man restrained from rising, a man lying on the ground as if dead. In our barracks and bivouacs we share the soldiers' meal, blood and oaths, in Rome as in Dalmatia, in Britain as on the shores of the Black Sea. Foot-sloggers, slingers, sappers, scouts, camel-troopers, tiro and veteran, in the stations of the night and scarred by old wounds we do not speak of what we have seen. If something has happened, it has happened between us. *Nama.* Shake on it.

The Founders of the City

They shared a birthday, blew its matching candles
out between them, flew their flag atop the capitol
to the rapture of the roaring crowd; elephants

hauled their juggernaut along the Via Salaria
and girls hurled bouquets of roses till the gutters
ran reeking red: the fur-wrapped princes swayed

and smiled. At the foundation of every empire
there it is, the old story read aloud in the nursery
by lamplight, how the wolf tiptoed up to the palace

and nosed its way in while the moon was dark;
how it snatched the people's dream of peace and plenty
in its jaws, dragged the bloodstained coverlet

through the mud. A howl of Exocet sears the night –
the princes whimper in their sleep. Their wet-nurse
bares her teats and turns the page. Her lupine boys.

Nightingale with a Rose

Fresco, Pompeii

Deep in the afternoon, the sky turns to goldleaf –
feel now how easy it is to live in the flesh,
like wildflowers in a vase of river who spawn
their vivid greens and mauves as if there were only
beginnings, hedge-nests of fledglings on the brink
of becoming song. Your boys are out netting fish
in the brook, a neighbour is stooping inspectorily
over his vines, the ash cloud is still only a glint
in the eye of the mountain. You know if you look
what you will see. Such a glut of foxglove, kingfisher,
marigold, it could tear the heart out of you.
Getting up from your ledger, you'll step outside
for a moment to breathe the careless evening air,
its citrus, woodsmoke, everything you'll ever want.

Wallflowers

Fresco, Pompeii

You wash your hands too often, you can't sleep,
you bang and bang on the glass to be let out,
to be let in. Life's becoming dull and hard,
rage and guilt and dread, all the old undeads

slouching there with you at table drinking
your health in vinegar, Caesar's veteran alone
with the view of painted jays. The months
are long, hot, cloudless – so little shade

on the endless limestone road with its kill
blossoming in ditches. You're stifled, the mind
is the scene of crimes, you need a tabula rasa,

fresh start. Tear up the cypresses, pomegranate,
that kitsch asphodel. Then these to fill your eyes:
morning glory, dog-rose, plum, the *papaver somniferum*.

Dying Gaul: Abu Ghraib

The nape of the neck is the sweet spot,
the point when the spine surrenders
and the crouched fist of the heart unfurls
as cadenza, lament. In the prime of his life

the statue he makes of himself is the one
we can't touch, the ballet his body performs
as he's falling, felled by the light coming
down on him. How has it come to this,

the stripping and cuffing? The whole world
has tipped, a house with its roof blown off,
no moon or stars in the dome over his head.
We can't take our eyes from his nakedness,

how endlessly he hangs there glimmering
in the gaol of our minds, the hood and leash
holding us closer and closer, not letting go.

Asylum

'ipse subibo umeris nec me labor iste gravabit'

The young women here are headscarved and majestic
and they drive like fury along the city's unmade roads.
Do they, in the marrow of their quick bones, remember

how one night they were hoisted on their fathers' shoulders
and the blanket that was flung over their sleepy dark heads
like another dusk? How not so long ago a man ran and ran

through the ruinous flames, and on his back his own father
still clasping the household gods to his shrunken chest
in case one day there would be a home again to put them in,

not a burnt-out truck or fenced-in camp on the edge of town,
but honey-cakes and thick coffee, the evening star to steer by?

A Story of Blue

*'Cum cernatur, nigrum, at in diluendo mixturam
purpurae caeruleique mirabilem reddit'*

There's a colour at the back of things
sombre and shining – ceremonial sky, seas

of ripening wheat, a dolphin reconnoitred
through spume. The darkening surface of time

as it passes. The northerly sea-lanes,
sea-glass carved into currencies,

opportunity like a sail on the horizon.
The irises in a blond stranger's gaze,

his shoals of soft stinking cloth,
a new kind of blue that's been wrung

out of green, vegetal not heavenly.
A dyer's fingernails indelibly stained

the ultramarine of the veins on her hands.
The flung-out *ikats*. The distances.

Mare Nostrum

'Make sure you get some real open-water practice. The worst thing you can do is just jump in and start swimming.'

An odyssey we've learnt to call it as night pitches them into obscurity, toy boats belly-up in bits, adverts for a better life. Troy is far behind on the Turkish coast, Greece and Rome and Germany and Dover somewhere in the unpronounceable future. Children and babies sleep on mounds of luggage; a man is shouting I wish we'd all died back there in the flames: pious Aeneas – refugee, widower – cursing god between retches. Everything is wrapped in black plastic bin-bags to keep out the sea, and for the shopkeepers of Izmir life jackets provide an unmissable business opportunity. *In a wetsuit you should feel slightly vacuum-packed but not restricted.* Nobody knows if they will leave tonight or next week. Everyone here is waiting. *Lift your head as little as possible, otherwise your hips sink. Think crocodile eyes.*

Britannia Welcomes Caesar

'...he reached Britain with the first squadron of ships, about the fourth
hour of the day.'

Here is our garden. Its four walls enfold a pair of rose bushes
that let down a confetti of petals, white and red, and a pergola

in the shape of a castle-carrying elephant: we call it a rook.
The garden is a perfect circle, in each of its corners is a tree,

one for every month – as you see, it is surrounded on all sides
by white horses, its skies are full of swan-winged sailing-ships

and little dogs laughing. You'll find no gold in our folk tales,
only salt and beer and brass monkeys, a kilner of piccalilli

from Piccadilly. Do not ask about the severed head on a pole,
nor whose lilywhite faces float in the stale air of the turret,

why a girl arrived with a tiny bundle after dark and hurried away
with half her heart: this is what the butler sees while everyone's

out hunting the fox-deer-crocodile-snark. Our beach-belles
pay their pennies on the promenade to watch your imperial fleet

plough up the plage between the carousels of deckchairs – we'll spell
your funny foreign name in cockleshells, write you through our rock.

Agricola to the Britons

Behind you the iron waves and rocks
of land's-end, under your feet brute ling-bog
and everywhere you look my watchtowers.
I've acquired a reputation for butchery,

my name's a bone in the throats of you all,
I've laid Albion waste and call it peace.
Or so you say. History will know us
as the apple-growers, chutney-makers,

sowers of dog-violet and love-lies-bleeding,
in our orchards your great-great-grandsons
perched high among the starlings will fire
their toy bow-and-arrows, their wee catapults,

tinkers will lean their bikes thankfully against
the mistletoe'd trunks and think of us; call
us farmers. (Out in the badlands merlins roost
among sticks and stones, hatching the fall.)

Vindolanda

Lucius Castor to Aelia Domitia, greetings. I am longing to return. Our instructions are to load the wagons with hides. I would have already been to collect them except that I did not care to injure the animals while the roads are bad. Our son practises writing: 'Meanwhile rumour rushes on restless wings through the frightened town'. I was unable to complain to the prefect because he was detained by ill-health. The mist has come down again, preventing any thought of departure. We pray that you are in good health. The Britons are unprotected by armour, but there are very many cavalry. Give greetings also to. This is written in haste. My dearest soul.

Mons Graupius

At some point we lay down on our backs in the heather, exhausted and uncertain. They say we inflicted a decisive defeat on the insurgents. We had marched north on the narrow road along the valleys, working a fast dark tunnel through the grey-green summer, getting by on a campaigners' diet of horse-blood and shoe leather. This was a winnable war, they said. The maps got it wrong or pointed in opposite ways over a landscape of standing stones, hit-and-run ambushes. From the hill, in those last days of the season and the sun low in the sky, we could see out across open water, how it darkened and sparkled, before the mist rolled in.

Lost Legion

A snow of early blossom had settled overnight;
from the hilltop it looked like wreaths of breath or smoke

hanging there in the thatch of black branches
as if a small clan had upped and left an hour or so ago
taking care to tread in the hoof-tracks of cattle

and not stopping to extinguish its meagre fires.
Now the river valley was merely itself
and its grey sky-water, but something wasn't

right. Hard to put into words, though any soldier
worth his salt knows the feeling. This is a country
of bee-keepers and sedge-plaiters – no
gun-runners or war-mongers, only blacksmiths

minding their own business making wrought-iron scrolls
and ornamental peacocks, shoeing brewery mares.
The old unexploded ordnance is up on the high peak
where no-one cares to go any more.

When it does come, it's done by stealth and betrayal,
there will be no other story.
Caesar's speech-writers will use the word *atrocity*.

Meanwhile the makeshift hamlets with their dead heroes
and evergreen hatreds have melted westward
into the wilderness: *gooks, towel-heads, Brittunculi.*

War wives jostle ghostlike at the edge of fields,
their rain-swept postures a landslide of grief.

Sculpsit

Fragment 1600 in city wall between west and south gates

Before anything else,
in broad-brush whitewash
paint her name, its slants

and uprights – angle
is everything. Then find
the rhythm, so the mallet

knocks like the beat
of a heart, yours, hers.
The chisel's metal bites

on limestone, setting
your teeth on edge
with the petrifying thicks

and thins of it, splinters
of rock fly like confetti,
serifs and glyphs

beginning to glint
in the glacial Britannic sun.
You spell her out

letter by perfect letter
carved and kerned to fit
the space you've kept for her

...ULIA... ...ILIA...
her VIXIT ANNOS XXX
waiting in the stone.

City of the Caesars

We walked towards it across a stubbled field,
visitors landing mapless in a foreign country.
The path curved upwards for a while, veered
off into an open sky. And then the past

re-appeared without warning, right on top of us,
blanketing our heads with the vast fall
of its shadow. The doorway was on the far side,
we'd to duck into its dark like old folk in a tale,

knees and elbows tunnelling through the fell.
The bare room smelt of sour earth, earth and staleness
– no hallucinogens, rites of passage, sad confetti.
Everything ends here, in aorist and dust:

full-stops of pollen-grain, skin-cells of dead things.
A place to be buried, not remembered, in.

Torc

When they came to the place again, it was not itself,
the road had been camouflaged with bines: soft April
explosions of cress and hogweed and oxeye, a bunker

for muntjac and boar. Perhaps, as they said, the hare
had really leapt out of her breast, screaming as it went,
its huge flamey ears ablaze in the sun: London

razed, the emperor's brazen head lolling in mud,
run hare run. But the field here's too narrow, the road's
heaving with iron and leather and sweat – the hare

zigzags in front of the eagle, wooden wheels trundle
hopelessly forward. (A hail of wild blossom shook
from the trees as the teeth of the harrow bit gold.)

Liddell & Scott, Lewis & Short

'...the simple and certain explanation is that Mr. Tomlinson
has confused the words "bangles" and "bugles" and does not
know what a demijohn is.'

Thick as bibles, they flumped
their ton of tissue-paper leaves

across the teacher's table, fell open
at the page of closely-printed scripture

that would deliver us from the sin
of ignorance. Eyeing the closed books

of epic, lyric, prose, we'd confuse *mori*
with *morari*, muddle *nox* and *mox*

the way sailors may mistake a cloud
for land; we navigated blind

through archipelagos of text, lagging
behind when we might have died,

longing for night that couldn't come
too soon. The lexicons corrected us,

we'd no idea then how far off-course
those gentlemen had veered,

how all at sea: *vide* errata, corrigenda,
addenda, supplement, multiple revisions;

and now the new editions, digital, Kindle,
fly the lawyer and Lieut. Col. worldwide

while inside my old cracked tomes
frowsty bookmoths, pressed to wisps,

have made digammas of themselves –
ghosts of vast lost tracts, *mortalia*, mist.

Kennedy's Revised Latin Primer

for Cynthia Royle

No-one wants to be left behind, trapped
in dull green buckram, the home-made jacket
of brown wrapping-paper worn and furred –
I suppose I must make a new edition of myself

or else inhabit that recurring dream of waking
as an exile in my own country, its syntax
sticking to my teeth; dragged back inside
the classroom to scan the unseen passage,

Vergil or, worse, Propertius, summer term's
windows open to mown grass and vast light
while Miss Royle waits. '*Oratio obliqua*'
I hazard, gazing at all those subjunctives

that suggest the question is not rhetorical;
while behind other doors states of matter
are being parsed into air and particles of dust.
Years move through our lives in logarithms,

acres of playing-field translate into highway,
their beauty taken, by fire, by rain.
Now the pluperfect begins to write our lives,
how could we think such languages are dead?

Mood

This was advanced study, had me secretly leafing
    to the end of the primer for the quiet nobility
of supines, the weatherproof posture of locatives:

voices in the road, the straight street that runs out
    to the provinces, rain-pocked sea always beyond,
infinite. An up-torn whinbush, a scuff of chalk

in the turf are indicative. The army skidding round,
    hooves stammering on stone. Imperative
to get the advantage – scouts grubbing in the grass

for particles of knowledge, nothing in themselves
    but huge with meaning in the right place. Like this
votive offering, a springtime scene not hard to parse,

this optative with its gaping throat and caved-in skull
face-down in a fen: wishful thinking made brute fact.

Her Cock-a-Doodle-Do

Bronze figurine in the shape of a cockerel
decorated with coloured enamel,
first half of 2nd century CE

She was buried with her boots
for the long walk home, a bowl
to hold some honey cakes, and this:

a hackled, wattled thing that clucks
and waltzes, a yard-bird,
a scrapper. She caught a palsy,

the measles, malaria. Her parents
wail out her name, place coppers
over her eyes, give her small bones

to the grave. Spreading his feathers
a redcap struts on the headstone,
brings the rooftree down with his cries.

Millefiori

With the occupation came the blowers
of glass, and when the soldiers left
and the fortresses fell they stayed on,

fetched their pipes and aprons, set up shop.
Came earthquakes, house-fires, another
war, fifty. After the city was blitzed,

trade stopped. In the trample, bones
became eggshell, skulls became bowls,
glass a luxury none had seen; and soon

they grew used to the dark. Rescue came
late. At last, it was lifted clear from the muck,
and the light shone through. Then we knew.

Ware

'MARGARITA FUI'

Today the river shines like a pearl. Do not be fooled.
This is the cup from which ashes are drunk.
The way to the dead house is under these arches.

You may not take photographs. Wrap your self
in a grey grief you do not yet feel. Darken
until you can hear the bell under your skin.

The black vase and the red are gate-guardians,
cherishers of empty. Can you feel yet the unstable
china of your wrists? Is this slip of earth a child?

See, the doves are all asleep, quartz and porcelain.
Walk this way, anthropomorph, open the lid
of your nothingness, the slab and coil of it, the pinch.

Vitrea

Blown breath; choreography of blow-pipe and tweezers, *flatu figurare*. O Chihuly, o Blaschka (son and father), o Ennion – you have made us strangers to ourselves, mass-produced and fragile. Lift this to your lips: flux-light of Venice and Jerusalem, molten giddy dust, every atom in the body an exploding star, our ethereal chandeliers, our singular eyes and manifold inflorescences, our voguish melancholy harps, our bath-house windows – how little survives. A forgetting of this kind will have the restorer patiently piecing us together: return of the repressed. We ring and tremble in her hands.

Provincia Nostra

for M.R.

Elephant country. See them through Roman eyes, tall as a marble arch, the inquisitive grey trunks tearing at saplings, the great flat feet tamping earth into road, the sidelong stare of *musth*. In our papier-mâché beast-masks you and I rampaged through the wildflower meadows, our latifundia, not pausing for bird-cherries or the thirteen desserts of Noël. Now it's a painters' landscape, felt-tips of cypresses and sunflowers, crimson capsicums, scarlet geraniums, tangerine fish; little howdahs of *terre verte*, sea and sky, *luxe, calme* and a flamingo sunset on the lagoon. We walked to the top of the town to admire the feral brush-work we'd done thirty-odd years ago but our house had gone. Two ochre hand-prints on a wall, *les yeux dans les yeux*. The shadowless southern light.

Sappho on Inishbofin

'... my once-black hair has turned white'

i. Sappho Goes West

Her eyelashes are wet
with spray, the breeze takes
her breath, her speech

brims with absence:
the stars have faded
my voice deserts me

I sleep alone...
It's dawn and she's sailing
into her own shadow,

the citrus-groves and heat,
the cicada-loud nights
as far ago now as childhood.

The water slops and heaves.
Quitting her father's house
she's crossed seven seas

to catch this glimpse of Inis Bó Finne,
isle of the white cow,
its great trembling body

afloat in a blaze of gold,
its craggy head lifting,
garlanded in haze, half-there.

ii. She Names the Flowers

Sappho is good at flowers.
Naming them, the verge flowers, vetch
and toadflax, fuchsia, hydrangea,

which hereabouts is mostly blue,
buddleia studded with butterflies, wild rose.
Like mother like daughter.

In her mind she holds the small hot hand,
points out the peat flowers, sedge
and bog cotton. Look she'd say look

the lough like glass, the water falling
and the hearth smoke rising,
peat smoke misting along the creek,

ghost among the goat-willows.
She'd plait her girl a cap of daisies,
compose the wall-breakers, saxifrage

and stone-crop, the grave lichens,
in the narrow fields bee orchid and harebell;
at the roadside famine flowers, gorse, thrift.

(Light swells and ebbs in restless currents
across the bay, rinses her. She begins forgetting
the headiness of *milk-white pansies, melilot*.)

iii. She Dances a Slip Jig

Friday night at Máire's Bar, ten o'clock
and the place is beginning to heave –
squeezebox and fiddle settling themselves,
bodhrán and whistle, bones and spoons.
She's the demure one sitting in a corner,
homespun skirts down to her toes, waiting
for the old music to waken,
the mandolin on her lap reminding her
of the (*songdelighting clearsounding*) lyre
she left behind. Always it starts slow and silky;
then the rhythm picks up, hickory tipper
on goatskin, nine–eight time and then some,
a fig for a kiss and they're all on their feet
and dancing, yes, *dance like a wave of the sea.*
And suddenly she's leaping bare-armed
through the jingling courts of herself
and the women are shrieking like banshees
– *Eavan, Eiléan, Nuala, Medbh* –
urging her on with their mouth-music,
but the *sean-nós* in her ears is all Greek,
snatches of exile-song, torn shreds
of voice, lambs' wool on blackthorn;
then a dog barking at the brotherless moon
and the last house light put out.

iv. She Meets the Bog People

She's looking through glass
at the barley-eaters,
the ginger-haired, the slain,

staring at their shut faces,
the tanned hide of their thighs,
their perfect nails. Her gaze

makes sons and husbands of them,
these ruined bridegrooms
wedded to the wet heart of the bog.

O, she has sailed all the way for this –
such cold enthralment,
such terrible splendours.

v. She Rents a Bothy

Coming back from the dead
Sappho shrugs on her winter coat
and packs a haversack: she's working

on a theory of memory, how it carries
the call of a wee bird tseep-tseep
like a solitude within it, how it returns

in summer with its gold eyes, how it flies.
Less than a day and a ferry-ride later
she'll be standing on the dark earth

three thousand miles from home
– but if she turns the map sideways
her tin shack will sit at the hub of the world

and the racing weathers of the self,
she'll read the etiquette of fuel and refuse,
of well-water and burial of excrement,

she'll light a candle, set a jar of wildflowers
on the single sill. The moon will be
the colour of a mussel shell.

vi. … and Prepares a Meal for Her Guests

Moments before the first knock on the door
and the antique moon rising in the pane,

she's forgotten who was invited.

Apples ripen and soften in candlelight, their seeds
swelling a little and a little in their star chambers.

The salt-crusted garden is asking to be let in,

wants to know if the table is set with the old silver.
Four chairs are standing round with their arms open.

She turns up the flame and waits.

vii. She Swims with Dolphins

Some say horsemen, some say warriors,

or the wake of shining ships, are the loveliest things.
Sappho begs to differ. This island now

is all she wants, its dazzle and drizzle, its restless

waters, its three drowned boys
looking north. The tide is where she belongs.

She dives, pouring herself into the roar and rush,

the icy gasp, the undersong. She's not alone.
She's finned and swarthy, a stranger to herself,

a lissom child flying to its mother.

She feels the slant light stroking her wrists,
the warmth beneath the wave-chill:

creature-comforts, soul-waters.

viii. Her Theory of Memory

The theory: I loved you, Aoife, once.
Aeons ago. My nights are long,

this heart-heaviness a memento
of the lily-of-the-valley you wore, our soft bed,

and how I wanted to die.
Memory: my tears. Your smile.

ix. Sappho and the Hag of Beare

Sappho's bones are aching. Ouf.
She feels as old as time. Crabby.

She's been sitting for hours –
one of those slow August evenings –

on a folding chair among the lettuces,
a shroud of carpet round her shoulders

staring sightlessly at the wild swans
and the rain-soaked light.

She coughs and spits into a used tissue.
Shrinks inside her leathers,

an auld bog-body,
all wantonness gone –

sine mé ná an Chailleach Bhéarra
I am older than the Old Woman of Beare...

She turns her face to the low sun
and the place where the wild rose-hips will come.

x. Sappho Has the Last Word

Across a troubled grey ocean
the signal comes and goes

lilting and lurching,
picking up sounds of remembrance,

an electricity of homesickness and want,
sparks in the welter of darkness:

my love has fared inland
it might say, or equally

and I would have gone with her anywhere
or – with that same undercurrent

of bitter-sweetness –
I thought about the hare, in her hour of ease.

Such a presence in the mouths of women
as if the sea had spoken in you

or the island suddenly reappeared
in its pure glass aspect

but earthly as rain or fields,
a furnished in-dwelling, a haunt of words.

III.

'And the smoke of it
fragrant with spices'

Alcuin's Nightingale

'e li aucel
chanton, chascus, en lor lati'

Clad in its bird robes a small soul
perches in the night-tree, waiting to enter –

the windows of the senses can be slow to open.
Evening has stolen another day

and soon the concert-halls fill with shadows;
under her basque and fishnet the jazz-singer

is a muscle of music, her solar plexus
a membrane between worlds: wold and sky,

thunder and lilacs. The bird in her throat
rhymes sweetness with sorrow and at his desk

a poet weeps because he has no Latin,
the words for love-song, life-long, loss.

Michaelmas

for Peter Dronke

Plebs angelica
the Alcuins and Angilberts
male voice choirs
phalanx et archangelica
in this packed golden room
are ventriloquised
from the bowed dark head
of our tutor whose
faint Rhenish accent
proposes a philology of song
seraphim si voce tonantem
as I stare out of a window
lost in unholy longings
delicias mundi, dulcia
iuventutis and having no
excuses but the sycamore trees
which are pricking my eyes
de ramis cadunt folia
with this radiance of feathers
and like love on its long way down
through winter's cadences
sola ego caleo

Alcuin Crosses the River

'A man and a woman of equal weight, together with two children, each of half their weight, wish to cross a river using a boat which can carry only the weight of one adult...'

Turbulent the waters by the willow-banks
where a wooden boat waits, and a vole's snout

pulling the brown flood like a skein in the dark:
ideal conditions for crossing the river, proving

the rule. The skiff holds two. There is no island
and all the husbands are jealous. How many

journeys to paddle each of their wives unsullied
to the other side? Or was it a wolf and a goat

and a sack of kale, oddest of fellow travellers
for a knight of the road? Two boys, their canoe

and three rookies desperate to come home?
What can the answer be but the spirit's voyage,

a rickety bridge lit by a single lamp – the flame
smokes and flutters. The children are borrowed,

as all children are, lent for a season, bright-eyed
and salvific as psalms, lighter than feathers, heavier

in their parents' hearts than a cargo of lead.
They would steep their own bodies' bones

in this torrent if the girl and boy would flower
and thrive. Alcuin takes the oars in his papery hands,

hell-bent on delivering these four bare souls
to a jib of land, inventing a simple algebra of love.

Tempest

beats with all its bared fists
against the window, a reckoning
whose time has come or will
as if a dead language wants to
speak again and soe the flodde

comes to cover the londe fram
Wealingaford and Readingum
to Scepertune, Stanes, Wyndleshora,
Wyrardisbury, Colebroke,
Cerotisege, bailing over banks

and sills a shit-lake withouten ende.
The discipuls tak frit, salva nos
maegester Iesu! and he respondit
quid timidi estis myne sparwes?
Benedicite drowned dogs, rats,

cattle, benedicite Black Datchet!
Et venti et mare obey him, god
of sewers and silverfish,
none speaking what is sooth:
man is vera causa of bad weather

Saint

'Do you not know that you are each an Eve? You are the devil's gateway...'

'Make us, O Lord, to flourish like pure lilies in the courts of Thine house...'

It is her age of iron. A tin of water,
a fist of bread are pushed at her
through the gap in the wall. Her skirt

is tidemarked with piss, o where is your mercy?
The sky trembles as dusk comes,
the woman's hour, with its veils and birdcalls,

and on the stones a faint mantling of rose.
But this is not the real house of horrors,
the one made of mouths and glistening hair

where the men live, burning, frozen;
remembering her inventive embroideries,
the wine in the blood, the scent of her,

the breakable bread of her body, all
her soft technologies. Nightly they pray for her.
She sings at them like an animal, an angel.

Monster

I'm sweating like a fountain in the oven of these back streets,
my master uses me on market days to tell fortunes.
I could tell yours, little pretty one, easy as winking –

look in the mirror, there's a dainty face floating
above all those pots of kohl and cloves and otto of roses,
you look pleased with yourself and your daring marriage

(bales of Shantung silks, tea-crates, wickers of limes,
Indian tamarinds candied in jars, all piling up on the quay
as we talk, your husband gulping iced sherbet,

shouting for a scented towel to mop his forehead, suddenly
daydreaming of his unborn black-eyed son). Oh and here's me
peering over your shoulder, hollow-cheeked and hang-jawed,

ugly as sin you'll tell your maid, and my stare is pale
like the devil's. My mother wept when I was born. A female
as monstrous as I is a mirror of the world's soul

says my master the philosopher – people see themselves
in me more truly than before, like puppets in the cosmic Eye.
Meanwhile he measures my pox-pitted skull, siphons my fluids,

calibrates the webs between my fingers. Scribbles in a book
he locks away. I tell him stories. Things I've heard. Not all
your children will take after your husband, they say. Unburden

your troubles, sister, all your pricking secrets: we're the same age
though my skin's as dry as a currant. I must earn my keep
and from now on you'll need to buy those nights of dreamless sleep.

The Desert Fathers

'These men, by the very exaggeration of their lives,
stamped infinity on the imagination of the West.'

Out they go from their offices at the appointed hour
and as they reach the street they do not turn to give
one last look at the vanishing shoreline of their careers

but carefully set their bin-bags against the plate-glass wall
where clouds pass by on their way out to sea: the sacks
are stuffed with old files, shucked books and a drift of photos

of summer-clad children who, gazing out from their mothers'
eyes, had graced each desk alongside the calendar-clock
and copies of cadastral maps. And now they make their way

in silence to the edge of town where the lost souls of dogs
cough and bark at faint stars, mistaken for strangers. At home
tables stay laid for the suppers they will not sit down to,

bedclothes unslept in, keys unturned in the lock, while they
are toting their bodies like begging bowls, full of labour
and wanting, towards the undying plenty of stony places,

intimates under a black sky and its flights of insects singing
of spiritual hunger. The noise of their nights is deafening,
the moon's fortissimo blaze drowned in the locusts' endless

recitation of scriptures. The new arrivals bathe their feet
in dust, replenish themselves on desolation. They walk on
into the exalted parch of those oceans, walk and never stop.

Lent

for Mary Atkins

At each window sits a woman in waiting.
In a few weeks she must write all she knows.

This is the clay house, the house of souls
for whose safe passage anxious prayers

are privately heard. In the pearly morning mist
how pale the garden is, all its mouths glisten

like grails. How could she guess these are
the *très riches heures*, the borrowed years?

Nominy-Dominy

'Latin is for skulking in.'

When does a language come back from the dead? With the well of baby-bones under a bathhouse (the cleft palates and polydactylics, the anencephalics and intersexes, the still-borns and abortions); the verdict of dolus eventualis on the far side of a bathroom door; the alias and alibi, the hocus pocus and the M.O.? Or the priest-holes and wind-chimes, the shadow of an eagle on the hill-field, paradise always already lost, ora pro nobis post cibum et hora somni? Yes, all these undead. Yet what does Latin know even now of the far north, bleached and sinless, its haecceitas and quiddity, its mosquitoes and wordless singing? Lully lullay and deo gracias bye bye. Meanwhile we practise our paternosters among the rose-trees like a form of tai chi, solvitur ambulando, the whole nominy-dominy.

Truce

It begins with olive branches, candles unofficially placed in the stricken trees, then hollered greetings and the exchange of small gifts in the nowhere and everywhere, the between-time when, all colour having fled, the world turns austere and potent. A meal is served, a dish for each disciple: cabbage soup, smoked eel, kartoffelsalat, candied quince, et cetera. Now and here, a brief peace exists between friend and foe, god and man, settler and wolf, sun and moon; they hold their collective breath as the dead are put in earth and a newborn bursts raw and gasping in the smash and grab of incarnation. Swaddling bands are shrouds-in-the-making, each crib's a tomb; at the crack of the year, Quempas and Paramony and the funeral games. Processional flame of torches along the shore. Then Aeneas, weeping, cuts down the first oak for a pyre, opera atque labores.

Oratio Obliqua

'Remember that these are guidelines; you may encounter oddities in original texts.'

Overheard in the heilige nacht, the voices of the normally inaudible, free indirect speech like the sea of galilee in your ear – silkie, mothman, cockatrice, hedgehurst, townies yearning to become their true beast-selves verbum caro factum through bray and bleat, blart and bellow, beat-box nonce-words: what manner of subtle salutation. And now it's the brutes' turn, their throat-sung voices huge and strong a capella da capo eia popeia angels all with their theriomorphic masks on, every last atom in the universe turning arsy-versy o wie lacht and nothing can ever be the same o wie lacht and so the handsome grey parrot no longer parrots but speaks, truth to power, hodie natus est, ohò. You be good, see you tomorrow. I love you.

The Court Poet Prepares to Take Leave of Her Lady the Garden

'Bella domna... a vos mas coblas man'

Lady since I must leave you let me leave you
these well-meant words
as courtesy demands

and my duty as the faithful scholar
of your weathers.
Let the poets praise

the perishable blush of your roses,
your herbal medicines,
the *flor* of your *cortezia*,

your processional gowns and scarlet.
I would have sung you
otherwise:

your gales that blew reckless spaces
intimately through me,
the single flowerheads

that hid in your grass, refined as geishas;
the rain-drenched gates
of your body,

your bones of glass, the small hard nipples
deep in your blossom,
I would have celebrated these.

Lady though you are full of gaiety and all good things
one could ask of a woman
I would have hymned

the ramshackle sheds of your sleep,
their owlish longings,
your bee-stings

whose tiny sacs are horned like human ovaries,
your bee-orchids
and orb-weavers

who with their pheromonal engineering
adorned you
on autumn mornings.

I would have crept inside the torn sleeves
of your hypotheses
concerning hybrids and survivors,

I would have brought you my daughter
who is like marigolds,
and with your trees

I would have spelled the year. I would have had the winds
play the harp
of your bravuras,

for you I would have recited the *benedicus benedicat*,
broken your first breads
then sung for my supper,

unable to accomplish with my faltering art
what my heart wanted.
So if one star-scented evening

you had caught yourself imagining a voice –
its tongue-tied syllables
no nightingale's –

and shaken out all your seed-purses to find it
I would have been glad.
I would not have looked back.

Arcady

'They lived like gods without sorrow of heart...'

i.m. Elizabeth Rawson

It's the soft things that perish first: the horse-hair
mattresses and the warm flesh that lay on them
in love's skilful luxury till late morning, the figs

and lavender bags, the sweet nothings – placated
indoor lives lived under damp thatch or sun-soaked canvas.
What lasts, their stone walls and stone floors,

their millstones, tombstones, flint-knaps, cannonballs,
green-glazed beads, have become the studied past.
All that remains of their gifted selves is a word, all that's left

of their words is a marble code, the start and end
of something untranslatable in another country,
but lucid as the deciduous rose-gold light on house-backs,

the view from an empty window to the southern peaks
and battlefields, as far as the shining tor and its sky
unfathomably, monumentally, blue.

English Heritage

'You will gaze upon the face of Agamemnon.'

Age is carved into the oak like a name
in a strange hand, hard to read in the dark
that lays its glove over our eyes as we walk
through the hall. The door is not locked,
though an intruder's footfalls would barely
be heard on the carpeted stairs. In place
of a cushion a single white rose has been left
on a chair, as if a husk of sky had dropped
all this way through the glass dome, chilled
the room to its bones. Someone has gone
without saying a word. We are here only once.

Ephemera

Islamic State beheaded Khaled al-Asaad, keeper of Palmyra's cultural artefacts, in 2015.

for Jo Balmer

Incarnation is hard for us all, the little daily ecstasies of the flesh, their grass-like transience, *terram corp[us] quae [dederit]*. Alexandria, Damascus, Aleppo, Palmyra, we are born idolaters making archives of ourselves – figurines, eye-miniatures, small vessels containing locks of once-bright hair, intimate visions, the jewel-encrusted look of love. We are an infidel tribe of philologues with our psalms and sutras and surahs hand-scribed on codices, tablets, scrolls, on birch-bark, silk, calf-skin, on tissue-thin paper in gold-tooled leather-clad perfect-bound books smuggled in saddle-bags to journey the globe, books of hours, books of the dead. Their capacity for decay, the inherent vice of things, is almost unbearable. Fanatics have an answer. Follow the paper trail, wisps and tittles of precious pages as tiny and light and white as olive-blossom.

The Farness of Latin

'Latin no longer says anything, or hides anything.'

i. Vagantes

Play-acting with a dragon-flag
a draggle of saddle-tramps
let go from the once-army

is still heading for the frontier
with a song and sixpence.
Post-war, Miles and Gloriosus

will sit in the Cat and Custard Pot
to dream of Istria, those distant
summer nights by the sea-pools,

the piss-ups, and hey do you
remember the way that hip-wagging
Syrian girl could shiggle her castanets?

ii. Carmina

All through the war and rubble
like a thrush's egg in a boy's palm

the secret romantic quality of Latin
somehow survives the marching

and manoeuvring, the out-flanking
and over-wintering, the wall-building

and hostage-taking, the vote-rigging
and land-grabbing, the flag-waving,

bean-counting, news-mongering,
the bath-housing, money-laundering,

tin-mining, oyster-fishing, snail-breeding,
the manumitting and fornicating,

and turns itself into a choir of birds.

iii. Provincia

An old house is leaking along the seams
of its skin, its flanks blackened

by shrill winters of Britannic sleet.
In this leafless glistening world

people are listening for the drip
and seep, the coming flood under the moon

that will buckle the great gold scriptures
into wordless dunes and mildews.

iv. Vera causa

gingiber, lilie, raedic, sioloc, coc, finugl:
how could the Saxons have coped

without the loan-words for ginger, lily,
radish, silk, cook, fennel, those basics

for a well-lived life? Or *engel*, angel,
candel, candle, *maegester*, master,

sock, bishop, butter, pope and cat?
It hardly bears thinking of. No Latin,

no deeds of the kings, no seven sleepers,
no Arch-Weeper, no mirror of fools,

no Philomel. In Latin Newton's 'if and
only if' is logic's gift; Otto's minstrels

sang in Latin to save him from the fire.
O table, by, with or from the table,

gingiber, lilie, raedic, sioloc, coc, finugl:
how lightly the door was flung open.

v. Latinitas

the Audibility of Latin
the Autobiography of Latin
the Causes of Latin

the Seaworthiness of Latin
the Long-beardedness of Latin
the Lorem Ipsum of Latin

the Birdsong of Latin
the Femininity of Latin
the Violence of Latin

the Julyness of Latin
the Pageantry of Latin
the Patience of Latin

the Iridescence of Latin
the Farness of Latin

vi. Consolatio

Another cell another emperor
palm under the heel of the jawbone
parchment laid across the knees

a table-cloth for spilled prayers
– how little our lives are
how green the chant of rain

in the service-tree and how strong
the heart of the faraway brother
who comforts our unloveliness

The New Troy

'We are committed to preserving our ancestral ethnic and cultural heritage.'

'Let the Britains descent stand good, as they deduce it from the Trojans.'

It depends how far back you want to go. To the admirable ancient Greeks for example whose hegemonic gaze nailed the Trojans as forever-Other – they smelt strange, spoke strange, knelt before strange gods. *A swarm of people coming across the Mediterranean seeking a better life*, perfect barbarians. Surviving shipwreck, slavery they find a place to land Lesbos Lampedusa Torbay somewhere to call home. The chilly island they'll risk their lives to reach is rich in greenwoods full of game, rivers teeming with trout – not their own nation of bee-eaters and bulbuls, temples and alabaster figurines, saffron and damask rose; but their mission is to civilise. And from Brutus the Trojan come Lud and Lear and Cymbeline and Old King Cole, King Arthur, a deuce of Queens Elizabeth, the whole Poly-Olbion, the best of British.

Notes

The Vergilian epigraph, from Book VI of the *Aeneid,* was translated by Seamus Heaney as: 'On they went then in darkness, through the lonely / Shadowing night, a nowhere of deserted dwellings'.

Oxyrhynchus
The much-quoted epigraph is from the novel *Requiem for a Nun* by William Faulkner.

Terrorist
'polyphloisboio thalassēs', a phrase recurring in Homer, means 'of the loud-roaring sea'.

Fray
The Homeric virtues are *aidōs* (duty), *arētē* (military virtue), *kleos* (glory), *mētis* (intelligence) and *timē* (prestige).

A Private Woman
The epigraph is taken from Roberto Calasso's book *The Marriage of Cadmus and Harmony*. The poem's title is taken from a description by Elizabeth Riggan of Helen Ede, wife of the artist Jim Ede:

> On a clear spring afternoon, light floods through windowpanes washing the surfaces throughout Kettle's Yard with a warm glow. Through the cottage and up to the top of the staircase, we come to Helen Ede's sitting room, bedroom, and bathroom. Mrs. Ede was a private woman; it was not very often that she engaged with visitors, therefore her bedroom and bathroom were the only spaces of the house that remained closed to guests during the years of the Ede's residence.

Her husband once wrote of her: 'She believed that she no longer desired the love of men' (in *Savage Messiah*) – which chimes with Calasso's description of Helen of Troy as living, after the fall of the city, apart from the company of men. On one of the walls in Helen Ede's bathroom is a calligraphy of a verse from Psalm 68: *'Non me demergat tempestas aquae neque absorbeat me profundum'* [o let the storm of water not drown me nor the deep make me its own]. In the poem

I've replaced this with translated lines from Book V of Homer's *Odyssey* (lines 419–20); the other quotation is from Book III of Homer's *Iliad*, line 392 (both from the Loeb bilingual editions).

Helmet
The epigraph is from Book VI of the *Iliad*, line 472, and means 'and forthwith glorious Hector took the helm from his head' (Loeb bilingual edition).

Shield
The epigraph is a line spoken by James Bond in the film *Casino Royale*.

Olfactory
The epigraph is from a speech by Philoktetes in the play of the same name by Sophocles.

Nociception
The epigraph is from another speech by Philoktetes in the same play. The poem was occasioned by a radio programme on how sufferers of chronic pain are being encouraged to describe their feeling of pain.

Sack
The phrases in Latin are taken from Book II of the *Aeneid* by Vergil.

Assay
The epigraph is a remark attributed to Heinrich Schliemann when he discovered the cache of artefacts known as Priam's Treasure.

Trophy
The epigraph refers to a famous photograph taken in 1874.

Immortal Daughters
The epigraph is from Dioscorides' testimony to the lasting power of Sappho's poetry (unattributed translation).

Landfall
The epigraph is from a newly-discovered poem by Sappho, known as 'The Brothers', and means 'Charaxus has arrived! / His ship was full!' (translated by Christopher Pelling).

Mare Internum
The epigraph is from 'Ghostwritten Classics' by Edmund Richardson, in *Deep Classics: Rethinking Classical Reception*, edited by Shane Butler.

Praise Song for a Pair of Earrings
The epigraph is from *Homeric Hymn V*, *'To Aphrodite'*, lines 166–7 (translated by Hugh G. Evelyn-White).

Genestho
The epigraph is from a royal ordnance [papyrus no. Berlin P 25 239] granting tax exemption to Publius Canidius, an associate of Mark Antony; the word at the foot of the text, *genestho* or *ginesthoi*, was probably written by Queen Cleopatra VII herself.

Prosopography
The epigraph is from *The World of Odysseus* by M.I. Finley.

No-Name
The epigraph is from the words of the artist Lorna Graves, quoted in *The Independent* in connection with her work 'Burial Ground', described in the article as 'an enigmatic collection of vessels and effigies suggestive of Bronze Age grave goods'.

The Uses of Greek
The epigraph is from *On Flirtation* by Adam Phillips.

In section v., φευ της βροτείας φρενός means 'alas the mortal heart' (Euripides).

In section viii., lines 6–14 are the whole of Fragment 21 in *Sappho*, edited and translated by D.A. Campbell (Loeb bilingual edition).

Part II
The title of this section means 'Sea Coasts' and is also the name of a poetic treatise by Avienus (*fl.* 4th century), which includes references to the islands of Ierne (Ireland) and Albion (Britain).

Asylum
The epigraph is from Book II of Vergil's *Aeneid,* line 708, and means 'I will take you myself on my shoulders and the task will not weigh heavy on me'.

A Story of Blue
The epigraph is from Pliny the Elder's description in his *Naturalis Historia* of indigo and means 'To the eye it is black, but when diluted it gives a marvellous mixture of purple and sky-blue'. Pliny mentions that India – hence 'indigo' – is the source of the dye, imported via the Silk Roads.

Mare Nostrum
The epigraph, along with the italicised phrases in the poem, is from a leisure supplement in *The Guardian Weekend*, January 2016. Mare Nostrum – one of the Roman names for the Mediterranean sea – was a naval and air rescue operation operated by the Italian government to assist migrants crossing the sea to Europe from Africa and the Middle East.

Britannia Welcomes Caesar
The epigraph is from Book IV of *The Gallic Wars* by Gaius Julius Caesar (in a 19th-century translation).

Lost Legion
Brittunculi, a word written on a Roman tablet found at Hadrian's Wall, means 'wretched little Britons'.

Sculpsit
The epigraph is an item in *Roman Inscriptions of Britain: Bath* by R.G. Collingwood. *'Vixit annos XXX'* means 'she died aged 30'.

Liddell & Scott, Lewis & Short
The title refers to the standard lexicons for Ancient Greek and Latin respectively. The epigraph is from 'Notes on Lewis and Short' by R.L. Dunbabin in *The Classical Review*, December 1934.

Kennedy's Revised Latin Primer
The italicised line is a translation of Sextus Propertius' *Elegies,* Book III, 2, line 23.

Ware
The epigraph is an epitaph on a wall in the 'Dead House' underneath Somerset House in London and means 'I was Margaret'.

Vitrea

flatu figurare, a phrase written by Pliny the Elder is his description
of glass-working in the city of Sidon, means 'forming with breath'.

Provincia Nostra

This was the Roman name for what is now the region of Provence
in southern France; it was the first Roman province north of the Alps
to be 'settled'.

Sappho on Inishbofin

The epigraph is a fragment (fr. 58) of Sappho's poetry. The italicised
lines in the final section are from Medbh McGuckian, Eavan Boland,
Eiléan Ní Chuilleanáin and Medbh McGuckian respectively.

Part III

The title of this section is from 'Sequence for St Michael' by Alcuin
of York (see below) (translated by Helen Waddell).

Alcuin's Nightingale

Alcuin of York (735–804 CE) was a poet, churchman and teacher:
his famous poem, *De Luscinia*, about his pet nightingale which had
been stolen can be read in many ways, perhaps as a meditation on
the loss of faith or love. The epigraph is from a love poem by Guillem
de Poitiers (1071–1127), the first troubadour, and means 'and the
birds / sing, each one, in their latin' (unattributed translation).

Michaelmas

The italicised phrases are from various poems in *Mediaeval Latin
Lyrics*, edited and translated by Helen Waddell.

Alcuin Crosses the River

The epigraph is from the textbook *Propositiones ad Acuendos Iuvenes*
by Alcuin of York (unattributed translation).

Saint

The poem commemorates the martyrdoms of Ss. Maria Aegyptica,
Pelagia, Thaïs and other women accused of being prostitutes. The first
epigraph is from *De Cultu Feminarum* by Tertullian, one of the early
Church Fathers (unattributed translation).

The second epigraph (part of a longer prayer in the Mozarabic Rite, whose beginnings date to the 7th century CE) is the opening of the school prayer of St Mary's Grammar School for Girls, Northwood Hills, where I began to learn Latin and Greek:

'Make us, O Lord, to flourish like pure lilies in the courts of Thine house, and to show forth the fragrance of good works and the example of a godly life, through Thy mercy and grace'.

The Desert Fathers
The epigraph is from *The Desert Fathers* by Helen Waddell.

Nominy-Dominy
The epigraph is from *Suspicion for 10 Voices*, a radio play by Mark Lawson.

Oratio Obliqua
The epigraph is taken from an online teaching resource by Robin Meyer.

The Court Poet Prepares to Take Leave of Her Lady the Garden
The epigraph is from a *canso* by the trobairitz Bieris de Romans (*fl.* first half of 13th century) and means 'Lovely woman... to you my stanzas go' (translated by Magda Bogin).

Arcady
The epigraph is from *Works and Days* by Hesiod (translated by Hugh G. Evelyn-White).

English Heritage
The epigraph is from 'Ghostwritten Classics' by Edmund Richardson (see above).

Ephemera
The italicised phrase is taken from Ennius, 'the father of Roman poetry', whose work survives only in fragments; the whole phrase is *Terram corpus quae dederit ipsam / capere neque dispendi facere hilum*, which means 'And earth herself who had given the body receives it back and wastes nothing'.

The Farness of Latin

The epigraph is from *Latin or the Empire of a Sign* by Françoise Wacquet.

The reference in section ii to 'the secret romantic quality of Latin' is from the introduction to *Mediaeval Latin Lyrics* by Helen Waddell.

The New Troy

The first epigraph is taken from the website of Britain First, a British nationalist party founded in 2011. The second epigraph is from *Britannia* by William Camden (1551–1623), the first chorographical survey of the islands of Great Britain.